Getting to Know Me

Dialogues and Exercise
Workbook

(month/day)

1 2 3 7 16 35 71

(month/day/year)

TOMMIE A SHIDER

PAGE PUBLISHING, INC.
Conneaut Lake, PA

First originally published by Page Publishing 2021

ISBN 978-1-6624-4315-2 (pbk)
ISBN 978-1-6624-4316-9 (digital)

Printed in the United States of America

Acknowledgments

I wish to thank and acknowledge the New Brunswick School District for allowing me to touch so many lives of students, colleagues, and parents throughout my career.

I am grateful to my ESL family and colleagues: Leslie Katz, Anna Domolki, Harriet Karvasarsky, Andrea McLaughlin, Steven Macy, Gail Mitchell, Kathe Beegle, Marge Huber, Dr. Elsa M. Nunez, and in loving memory of Mrs. Joan M. Bornheimer for all their support and encouragement.

A special thanks to my publication coordinator, David Rodax. Your continuous support and assistance are greatly appreciated.

Lastly, this book is dedicated to all ESL students, teachers who use it to enhance their instruction, to my wife Diana Shider, children, Juan Carlos and Leslie Johanna Shider, and to the memory of my mother, Queenolia Shider.

Introduction

The *Getting to Know Me Dialogues and Exercise* book gets students talking and interacting!
   It teaches self-identification information using dialogues with follow-up practice dialogues and practical reinforcement worksheets.
   Units address school, family, work, friends, and favorites.
   Characters and visuals are infused to enhance comprehension.
   It provides oral presentations, as well as listening, reading, and writing exercises.
   The dialogues are written to provide an understanding of questions in various ways.
   Picture cards are included for the final unit: My Favorite Things.

Contents

Juan and Luz

A.

Juan: Hello!

Luz: Hello!

Juan: My name is Juan Ramirez. What's yours?

Luz: My name is Luz Colon.

Juan: Where are you from?

Luz: I am from Honduras. And you?

Juan: I am from Mexico.

Luz: Nice to meet you!

Juan: Nice to meet you too!

Luz: Where do you live?

Juan: I live at 111 Redmond Street New Brunswick, New Jersey. And you?

Luz: I live at 1018 Main Street Highland Park, New Jersey.

Juan: Well, I have to go. See you later.

Luz: See you. Have a good day!

Juan: You too.

B. Answer True or False.

1. Luz is from Mexico. _____
2. Juan lives in New Brunswick._____
3. Juan is from Mexico. _____
4. Luz's last name is Colon._____
5. Juan's address is 1018 Main Street. _____

C. Answer the questions.

1. Where is Luz from? _____
2. Where is Juan from? _____
3. Who lives in Highland Park? _____
4. Where does Juan live? _____
5. What is Juan's last name? _____

D. Answer the questions about yourself.

1. What is your name? _____
2. Where are you from?_____
3. Where do you live? _____
4. What is your first name? _____
5. What is your last name? _____
6. What is your address? _____

E. Practice the dialogue with *different* classmates and be prepared to present to the class.

A. Hello!

B. Hello!

A. My name's _____. What's yours?

B. My name is._____.

A. Where are you from?

B. I am from _____. And you?

A. I'm from _____.

B. Nice to meet you!

A. Nice to meet you too!

B. Where do you live?

A. I live at _____ _____ _____. And you?

B. I live at _____ _____ _____.

A. Well, I have to go. See you later.

B. See you! Have a nice day!

A. You too.

José

Teacher: Hello! My name is Mr. Jones. I am your teacher. What's your name?

José: My name is José Sanchez.

Teacher: Where are you from?

José: Mexico.

Teacher: What part of Mexico?

José: Puebla.

Teacher: What's your address?

José: I live at 686 Livingston Avenue, New Brunswick, New Jersey. Teacher: What's your age?

José: I don't understand.

Teacher: How old are you?

José: I'm twenty-one years old.

Teacher: Nice to meet you, José.

José: Nice to meet you too, Mr. Jones.

Teacher: See you tomorrow in class.

José: See you.

1 2 3 7 16 35 71

A. Answer True or False.

1. José is a teacher.   _____
2. Mr. Jones is a doctor.   _____
3. José is not twenty years old.   _____
4. José lives in Mexico.   _____
5. José is a boy.   _____

B. Answer the questions:

1. How old is José? _____
2. What is José's address? _____
3. Is Mr. Jones a student? _____
4. What is José's age? _____
5. Who is José's teacher? _____

C. Answer the questions about yourself.

1. What's is your age? _____
2. Where are you from? _____
3. What is your address? _____
4. Who is your teacher? _____
5. How old are you? _____
6. How are you? _____

D. Practice the dialogue with *different* classmates and be ready to present to the class.

Teacher: Hello! My name is _____. I am your teacher. What's yours?
Student: My name is _____.
Teacher: Where are you from?
Student: I am from _____.
Teacher: What's your address?
Student: I live at _____.
Teacher: What's your age?
Student: I don't understand.
Teacher: How old are you?
Student: I am _____ years old.
Teacher: Nice to meet you, _____.
Student: Nice to meet you too, _____.
Teacher: See you tomorrow in class.
Student: See you.

1 2 3 7 16 35 71

A. Directions: Fill in the missing words.

1. Where do you live? I live at _____.
    _____ do _____ live? I ____ at _____.
    Where ___ you ___? _____ live ____ _____.
    ____ ____ ____ ____? ____ ____ ____ ____ _____.

B. Put the question in order and answer in a complete sentence.

1. from Where you ? are
    Q. _____
    A. _____

2. do live ? Where you
    Q. _____
    A. _____

3. name your What ? is
    Q. _____
    A. _____

4. you How ? are
    Q. _____
    A. _____

C. Put the sentences in order.

1. from I Honduras . am

    _____

2. at 306 live Baldwin . I Street Brunswick in New

    _____

3. is Sanchez name My . Angel

    _____

4. meet to Nice ! you

    _____

Pablo and Veronica

A.

Pablo: Hey, Veronica!

Veronica: Hi, Pablo! How's everything?

Pablo: Just fine. What day is today?

Veronica: Today is Wednesday.

Pablo: Right! What is the date?

Veronica: It is January 29.

Pablo: That's right! Today is my birthday.

Veronica: Happy birthday, Pablo!

Pablo: Thank you.

Veronica: How old are you?

Pablo: I'm thirteen years old. I am now a *teenager*!

Veronica: Me too. I am fifteen years old.

Pablo: When is your birthday?

Veronica: My birthday is March 21.

Pablo: Well, I have to go now. I'll talk to you later.

Veronica: Bye, Pablo. Have a happy birthday.

Pablo: Thanks again.

(month/day)

B. Answer True or False.

1. Pablo is fifteen years old. _____
2. Veronica's birthday is March 20. _____
3. Pablo is a teenager. _____
4. Pablo's birthday is January 29. _____
5. Veronica is not a teenager. _____
6. Veronica is fifteen years old. _____

C. Answer the questions.

1. When is Pablo's birthday? _____
2. How old is Pablo? _____
3. When is Veronica's birthday? _____
4. How old is Veronica? _____
5. Whose birthday is January 29? _____
6. Who is fifteen years old? _____

D. Answer the questions about yourself.

1. How old are you? _____
2. When is your birthday? _____
3. Are you a teenager? _____

E. Practice the dialogue with *different* classmates and be prepared to present to the class.

A. Hello, _____!

B. Hi, _____! How's everything?

A. Just fine. And yourself?

B. I'm okay. _____, how old are you?

A. I am _____ years old. How old are you?

B. I'm _____.

A. When is your birthday?

B. My birthday is _____ _____. When is yours?

A. My birthday is _____ _____.

B. Well, I have to go now. I'll talk to you later.

A. Goodbye, _____.

B. Bye, _____.

1 2 3 7 16 35 71

F. Copy, study, and learn dialogue E

G. Fill in the missing words.

1. How old are you? I am _____ years old.

    How ____ are ____? I ___ ___ years old.

    ____ old ___ you? ___am _____ _____old.

    ____ ___ ___ ___? __ ___ ____ ____ ____.

2. When is your birthday? My birthday is _____ _____.

    _____ is _____birthday? _____ birthday ___ _____ _____.

    When ____ your _____? My _____ is _____ ____.

    _____ ____ _____ _____? _____ _____ ___ _____ ____.

H. Directions: Complete each sentence.

1. My birthday is _____ _____.
2. My name is _____ _____.
3. I am _____ years old.
4. I live at _____.
5. I am from _____.

I. Answer each question in a complete sentence.

1. Where are you from? _____.
2. When is your birthday? _____.
3. How old are you? _____.
4. Where do you live? _____.
5. What is your name? _____.
6. What day is today? _____.

Pablo and Mr. Jones

A.

Mr. Jones: Hi, Pablo!

Pablo: Hello, Mr. Jones! How are you?

Mr. Jones: I'm fine thanks, and you?

Pablo: I'm all right.

Mr. Jones: Pablo, you told me you are thirteen years old, right?

Pablo: That's right.

Mr. Jones: When were you born?

Pablo: I don't understand, Mr. Jones.

Mr. Jones: What is your date of birth?

Pablo: Now I understand. I was born on January 29, 1990.

Mr. Jones: What's your telephone number?

Pablo: My telephone number is (732) 418-6328.

Mr. Jones: Thanks for the information, Pablo. See you tomorrow.

Pablo: See you, Mr. Jones.

(month/day/year)

B. Answer true or false.

1. Pablo is fifteen years old. _____
2. Pablo was born on January 29, 1990. _____
3. Pablo is not a teenager. _____
4. Pablo's date of birth is January 29, 1990. _____

C. Answer the questions.

1. What is Pablo's telephone number? _____
2. When is Pablo's birthday? _____
3. What's Pablo's age? _____
4. When was Pablo born? _____
5. When were you born? _____
6. What's your telephone number? _____
7. What's your age? _____
8. What's your date of birth? _____

Note: When were you born? And what's your date of birth? Mean the same.

D. Complete the following sentences.

1. I _____ born _____ _____ _____ _____.

2. _____ name is _____ _____.

3. _____ am years _____.

4. I _____ _____ Colombia.

5. My birthday is _____ _____.

E. Answer each question in a complete sentence.

1. What is your first name?

   _____

2. When were you born?

   _____

3. How old are you?

   _____

4. What is your last name?

   _____

5. How are you?

   _____

6. What day was yesterday?

   _____

F. Directions: Fill in the missing information and read it to the class.

Hello!

My name is_____.

I am from _____.

I live at _____.

I am _____ years old.

My birthday is _____.

I was born on _____.

My telephone number is _____.

Reinforcement:

- Copy the sentences
- Say it *without* reading it.

Pedro and Mr. Jones

A.

Mr. Jones: Hi, Pedro!

Pedro: Hello, Mr. Jones! How are you?

Mr. Jones: I'm fine thanks, and you?

Pedro: I'm fine.

Mr. Jones: Pedro, what's your telephone number?

Pedro: My telephone number is (732) 418-5632.

Mr. Jones: What school do you go to?

Pedro: I go to Redshaw School.

Mr. Jones: What grade are you in?

Pedro: I'm in the sixth grade.

Mr. Jones: Who is your teacher?

Pedro: My teacher is Mrs. Sanchez.

Mr. Jones: Thank you, Pedro.

Pedro: You're welcome, Mr. Jones. Goodbye!

Mr. Jones: Bye, Pedro.

B. Answer True or False.

1. Pedro is in the fifth grade. _____
2. Pedro's teacher is Mrs. Sanchez. _____
3. Pedro goes to Roosevelt School. _____
4. Pedro does not have a telephone. _____
5. Pedro is not in the sixth grade. _____
6. Mr. Jones is Pedro's teacher. _____

C. Answer the questions about Pedro.

1. What is Pedro's telephone number? _____
2. What school does Pedro go to? _____
3. What grade is Pedro in? _____
4. Who is his teacher? _____

D. Answer the questions about yourself in complete sentences.

1. What is your telephone number? _____
2. What school do you go to? _____
3. What grade are you in? _____
4. Who is your teacher? _____
5. Who is your ESL teacher? _____
6. When were you born? _____

E. Find a different classmate to answer each question.
Write the name of the student you ask.

1. Who is your teacher?

   _____   _____

2. What grade are you in?

   _____   _____

3. What school do you go to?

   _____   _____

4. When were you born?

   _____   _____

5. Who is your ESL teacher?

   _____   _____

6. How old are you?

   _____   _____

7. What is your address?

   _____   _____

SHARE 3 ANSWERS WITH THE CLASS!

Directions: Circle and write the correct complete answer.

1. Where do you live?
   a. I live 24 Bayard St.
   b. I live at 24 Bayard St.
   c. Live at Bayard St.

   _____

2. How old are you?
   a. I am 15 year old.
   b. I have 12 years old.
   c. I am 12 years old.

   _____

3. What's your name?
   a. My name is Luz Colon.
   b. I am from Mexico.
   c. My is Luz Colon.

   _____

4. Where are you from?
   a. From Honduras.
   b. I from Honduras.
   c. I am from Honduras.

   _____

5. When were you born?
   a. I born May 5, 1971.
   b. I was born on May 5, 1971.
   c. My born is May 5, 1971.

   _____

6. When is your birthday?
   a. My name is Jose.
   b. My birthday is May 24.
   c. Today is Monday.

   _____

7. What is your last name?
   a. My last name is Juan.
   b. My last name is Diaz.
   c. My name is Maria.

   _____

8. What day is today?
   a. Yesterday was Monday.
   b. Today is Friday.
   c. Today will be Friday.

   _____

9. How are you?
   a. Fine, thank you.
   b. I am 13 years old.
   c. My name is Pedro.

   _____

10. What grade are you in?
   a. I am from Ecuador.
   b. I am 11 years old.
   c. I am in the fifth grade.

   _____

Directions: Write the question to the following sentences.

1. I live at 131 Seaman St. New Brunswick, New Jersey.

   _____

2. My name is Jorge Ramos.

   _____

3. I am ten years old.

   _____

4. My teacher is Mr. Jones.

   _____

5. I go to Lincoln School.

   _____

6. I am from Guatemala.

   _____

7. My birthday is August 12.

   _____

8. I was born on May 27, 1988.

   _____

9. I am in the eighth grade.

   _____

10. My last name is Aquilar.

   _____

More About Me

Situation: Mr. Jones (the teacher) asks Juan for information about his family.

Mr. Jones: Hello, Juan!

Juan: Hello, Mr. Jones. How are you?

Mr. Jones: I'm fine thanks, and you?

Juan: *Great*!

Mr. Jones: Juan, I need some more information about you.

Juan: Okay.

Mr. Jones: What are your parents' names?

Juan: My mother's name is Juana Sanchez, and my father is José Sanchez.

Mr. Jones: How many brothers and sisters do you have?

Juan: I have two brothers and one sister.

Mr. Jones: What are your brothers' names?

Juan: Pedro and Luis.

Mr. Jones: How old are they?

Juan: Pedro is eleven, and Luis is five.

Mr. Jones: What's your sister's name?

Juan: Her name is Ana. She's eleven too. Pedro and Ana are twins.

Mr. Jones: Really? What grade are they in?

Juan: They are in the fifth grade.

Mr. Jones: And Luis?

Juan: He's in the kindergarten.

Mr. Jones: Thank you, Juan, for the information. I'll see you tomorrow.

Juan: You're welcome, Mr. Jones. Have a good day!

Mr. Jones: You too!

A. Answer True or False.

1. Juan is a teacher.   _____
2. Juan's last name is Sanchez.   _____
3. Juan has two sisters.   _____
4. Juan's parents are his mother and father.   _____
5. His brothers' names are Luis and Pedro.   _____
6. His sister's name is Maria.   _____
7. Juan's mother's name is Ana.   _____
8. Luis and Pedro are not twins.   _____

B. Answer the questions in complete sentences.

1. What is Juan's father's name?

    _____

2. How old is Juan's sister?

    _____

3. Who is in the kindergarten?

    _____

4. How many sisters does Juan have?

    _____

5. What grade are the twins in?

    _____

6. How many brothers does Juan have?

    _____

C. Answer the questions about yourself?

1. What are your parents' names?

    _____

2. How many brothers and sisters do you have?

    _____

D. Practice the dialogue with *different* classmates.

A. Hello,
B. Hi, _____. How are you?
A. I'm _____ thanks, and you?
B. I'm _____.
A. What are your parents' names?
B. My mother's name is _____, and my father's name is _____, and yours?
A. My mother's name is _____, and my father's name is _____.
B. How many brothers and sisters do you have?
A. I _____. And you?.
B. I _____.
A. See you tomorrow.
B. Bye.

A. Directions: Fill in the missing words.

1. My parents' names are _____ and _____.

2. I have _____ brother(s).

3. I have _____ sister(s).

4. My mother's name is _____.

5. My father's name is _____.

B. Answer the questions in complete sentences.

1. What is your mother's name?

   _____.

2. How many brothers do you have?

   _____.

3. What is your father's name?

   _____.

4. How many sisters do you have?

   _____.

5. Who are you?

   _____.

6. What grade are you in?

   _____.

Old Friends

Situation: Pablo and Margarita are old friends. They meet each other downtown after not seeing each other for eight years.

Pablo: Hi, Margarita! How are you?

Margarita: Just fine, Pablo. Long time no see. How's everything?

Pablo: Not bad. It's good to see you again.

Margarita: Same here.

Pablo: What's new in your life? Are you married?

Margarita: Yes, I am. My husband's name is Miguel Galindo. How about you? Are you married?

Pablo: No, I'm not. I'm still single. Do you have children?

Margarita: Yes! I have two sons, David and Miguel, and one daughter, Sara.

Pablo: That's nice. How old are they?

Margarita: David and Miguel are nine. They're twins. Sara is five. Are you working?

Pablo: Yes. I work in the post office. I'm a mail carrier. And you?

Margarita: I'm a housewife. My children are still very young, so I'm not working now.

Pablo: Well, Margarita, it was great to see you again!

Margarita: Same here, Pablo. Take care and have a good day.

A. Answer true or false.

1. Pablo is married.   _____
2. Margarita is single.   _____
3. Pablo is a mail carrier.   _____
4. Margarita has two children.   _____
5. Margarita doesn't work.   _____

B. Answer the questions.

1. Who is single? _____.
2. Who has children? _____.
3. Where does Pablo work? _____.
4. How old is Sara? _____.
5. What is Margarita's husband's name? _____.

C. Answer the question about yourself.

1. Are you married?_____.
2. Do you have children? _____.
3. Where do you work? _____.
4. Are you single?_____.
5. What is your date of birth? _____.
6. When is your birthday? _____.
7. When were you born? _____.
8. How old are you?_____.

Question and Answer Session

D. Find a different classmate to answer each question below. Write the name next to the answer.

1. How old are you?_____   _____.
2. When were you born?_____   _____.
3. What's your address?_____   _____.
4. What is your last name?_____   _____.
5. Are you married?_____   _____.
6. What's your age?_____   _____.
7. What day is today?_____   _____.
8. When is your birthday?_____   _____.
9. Where are you from?_____   _____.
10. What's your first name?_____   _____.
11. What is your date of birth?_____   _____.
12. Where do you work?_____   _____.
13. Do you have children?_____   _____.
14. Where do you live?_____   _____.
15. How are you?_____   _____.

A. Directions: Fill in the blanks with your own information.

Hello! My name is _____. I live at _____

_____ in _____.
            (address)   (city / state)

I am from _____. I am (single/married).

I am _____ years old. My (husband's/wife's) name is _____.

I have _____ (child / children). I (don't) work _____.

My birthday is _____ _____.
                    (month)   (day)

I was born on _____ _____ _____.
                 (month)   (day)   (year)

My telephone number is _____. My parent's names are _____
                                                              (mother)

and _____.
    (father)

I have _____ brother(s) and _____ sisters.

My brother(s) name(s) is/are _____.

My sister(s) name(s) is/are _____.

B. Rewrite the entire paragraph on a sheet of paper.

C. Memorize and practice the paragraph for an oral presentation.

My Favorite Things

Situation: Juan and Paula practice English talking about their favorite things.

Juan: Hi, Paula! How's everything?

Paula: Just fine.

Juan: Let's practice English, okay?

Paula: Okay.

Juan: What's your favorite color?

Paula: My favorite color is blue. What's yours?

Juan: My favorite color is green.

Paula: What's your favorite day of the week?

Juan: Friday. What's yours?

Paula: Saturday.

Juan: What's your favorite music?

Paula: I love merengue. What's yours?

Juan: My favorite music is jazz.

Paula: What's your favorite holiday?

Juan: Christmas of course. What's yours?

Paula: I love Thanksgiving. I eat a lot on Thanksgiving.

Juan: What's your favorite season of the year?

Paula: My favorite season is spring because it's not too hot and it's not too cold. What's yours?

Juan: I love the summer. I enjoy the hot weather.

Paula: What's your favorite sport?

Juan: Soccer. What's yours?

Paula: I enjoy baseball. What's your favorite food?

Juan: Seafood. I love fish. What's yours?

Paula: Pizza.

Juan: Well, Paula, I have to go now. I have to work tomorrow.

Paula: Me too. It was great talking with you. See you tomorrow.

Juan: See you.

A. Answer True or False.

1. Juan's favorite color is green. _____

2. Paula's favorite music is jazz. _____

3. Paula and Juan like soccer. _____

4. Saturday is Juan's favorite day or the week. _____

5. Juan's favorite holiday is Christmas._____

B. Answer the questions.

1. What is Juan's favorite sport? _____
2. Who enjoys the hot weather? _____
3. What is Paula's favorite holiday? _____
4. Whose favorite food is seafood? _____
5. What is Juan's favorite color? _____

C. Complete the following sentences about your favorite things.

1. My favorite color is _____.

2. My favorite food is _____.

3. My favorite holiday is _____.

4. My favorite day of the week is _____.

5. My favorite music is _____.

6. My favorite season is _____.

7. My favorite sport is _____.

D. Answer the questions in complete sentences.

1. What is your favorite holiday?

   _____.

2. What is your favorite color?

   _____.

3. What is your favorite day of the week?

   _____.

4. What is your favorite season of the year?

   _____.

5. What is your favorite food?

   _____.

E. Practice the dialogue with a partner and present it to the class.

A. Hi, _____. How's everything?

B. Just fine.

A. Let's practice English, okay?

B. Okay.

A. What's your favorite color?

B. My favorite color is _____. What's yours?

A. My favorite color is _____.

B. What's your favorite day of the week?

A. _____. What's yours?

B. _____.

A. What's your favorite music?

B. I love _____. What's yours?

A. My favorite music is _____.

B. What's your favorite holiday?

A. My favorite holiday is _____. And yours?

B. I love _____.

A. What's your favorite sport?

B. _____. What's yours?

A. I enjoy _____. What's your favorite food?

B. My favorite food is _____. And yours?

A. My favorite food is _____.

B. Well, _____, I have to go now. I'll see you tomorrow.

A. See you.

Self-Identification Question/Answer Practice Sheet 1

Directions: Fill in the missing words. **Study** and **learn** each question and answer.

1. What's your name? My name is _____
   _____ your _____? My _____ is _____
   What's _____ name? ____ name is _____
   _____ _____ _____ ____ _____ ___ _____

2. Who are you? I am _____
   _____are ____? ____ am _____
   _____ _____ ____? ___ ___ _____

3. Where ____ you ____? I am from _____
   Where ____ you ____? I ___ from _____
   ____are _____ from? ___ am _____ _____
   _____ ____ ____ ____? ___ ___ _____

4. Where do you live? I live at _____
   Where ____ you live? I ____ at _____
   _____ do ___ live? __ live ___ _____
   ____ ___ ___ ____? ___ ___ ___ _____

5. What's you address? My address is _____
   _____ your ____? ___ address _____ _____
   What's ____ address? My _____ is _____
   ____ _____ ____? _____ _____ _____ _____

6. How old are you? I am _____ years old.
   ____ old ____ you? I ____ ____ years old.
   How ___ are ____? ____ am ____ years old.
   _____ ____ ____ ____? ___ ___ ___ ____ ___.

7. What's your age? I am _____ years old.
   What's ____ age? ___ am ___ years old.
   _____ your ___? I ____ ____ ____ old.
   _____ _____ ____? ____ ____ ____ ___.

1 2 3 7 16 35 71

1 2 3 7 16 35 71

33

Self-Identification Question/Answer Practice Sheet 2

8. What's your telephone number? My phone number is _____ _____ _____.
   _____ your _____ number? ___ phone _____ is _____ _____ _____.
   What's _____ telephone _____? My ____ number _____ _____ _____.
   _____ _____ _____ _____? ___ ___ _____ ___ _____ _____ _____.

9. When is your birthday? My birthday is _____ _____.
   _____ is ___ birthday? ____ birthday ___ _____ _____.
   When _____ your ____? My _____ is _____ _____.
   _____ ___ _____ _____? ___ ___ _____ _____ _____ _____ _____. (month/day)

10. When were you born? I was born on _____ _____ _____.
    When _____ you _____? ___ was _____ on _____ _____ _____.
    _____ were _____ born? I ___ born ___ _____ _____ _____.
    _____ _____ _____ _____? ___ ___ _____ ___ _____ _____ _____. (month/day/year)

11. What's your date of birth? My date of birth is _____ _____ _____.
    _____ your _____ of _____? My _____ of _____ is _____ _____ _____.
    What's ___ date _____ birth? _____ date ___ _____ is ____ _____ ____.
    _____ _____ _____ ___ _____? ___ ___ ___ ___ ___ _____ _____. (month/day/year)

12. Where do you work? I work at _____.
    Where _____ you _____? _____ work _____ _____.
    _____ do _____ work? I _____ at _____.
    _____ _____ _____ _____? _____ _____ _____ _____ _____ _____.

13. Are you married or single? I am _____.
    _____ you _____ or _____? _____ am _____.
    Are _____ married _____ single? I _____ _____.
    _____ _____ _____ _____ _____? _____ _____ _____.

14. Who is your teacher? My teacher is _____.
    _____ is _____ teacher? _____ teacher ____ _____.
    Who _____ your _____? My ____ is _____.
    _____ _____ ___ _____? _____ _____ _____ _____.

My Favorite Things Picture Cards

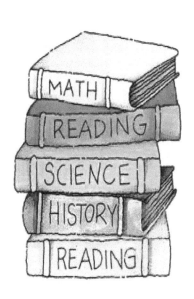

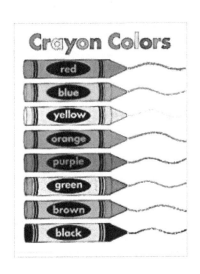

Colors

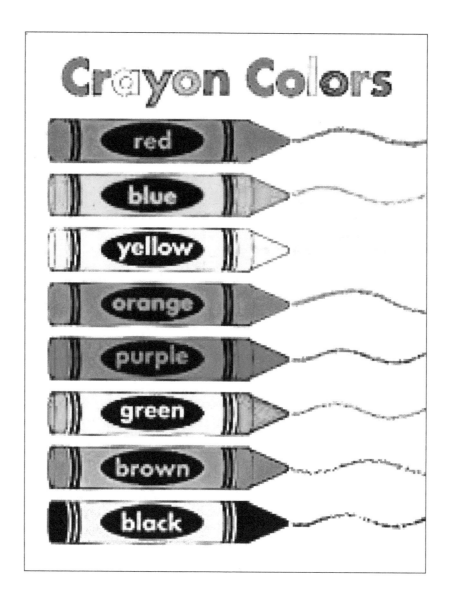

Days of the Week

Sunday

Monday

Tuesday

Wednesday

Thursday

Friday

Saturday

Music

Jazz

Hip-Hop

Rap

Reggae

Cumbia

Merengue

Classical

Doo-Wop

Food

Pizza

Chicken

Chinese

Fish

Vegetables

Seafood

Hamburgers

Soup

Eggs

Tacos

Hot Dogs

Holidays

Halloween

Valentine's Day

Thanksgiving

Patrick's Day

Christmas

Easter

Seasons

Sports

Baseball

Basketball

Tennis

Soccer

Football

Subjects

About the Author

Tommie A. Shider is a retired ESL instructor. He worked in the New Brunswick School District for thirty-seven years and has taught ELL students of all ages and backgrounds. He has also worked on the college level at Ramapo, Middlesex, and Union College.

During the last ten years of his career, he served as the ESL specialist in which he provided innovative teaching strategies and techniques, professional development, and workshops to colleagues, as well as to foreign teachers at the Rutgers PALS Program.

He received his bachelor of arts degree from Ramapo College of Mahwah, New Jersey, and his masters of education degree from Rutgers University in New Brunswick.

He is the creator of *Tommie's World*, where a little is a lot, and the author of four publications, *The Pronoun Book*, *ESL Reinforcement Activity Book*, *Survival and American Holiday Chants*, and *All About Me*.